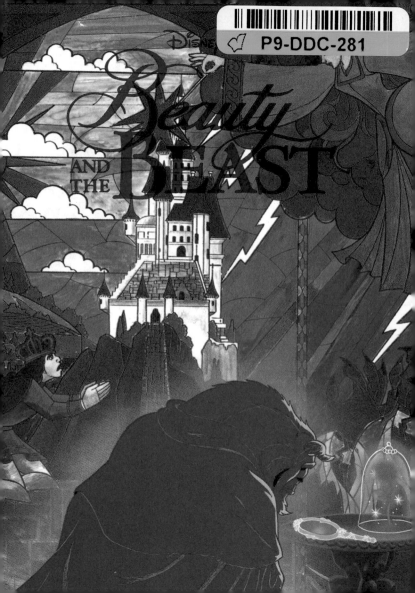

Once upon a time, a young prince lived in a shining castle. He was rich and handsome, but he had no love in his heart.

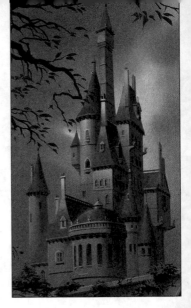

To punish him, an enchantress transformed him into a beast, and changed his servants into household objects. For the spell to be broken, the Beast needed to learn to love another, and earn that person's love in return. And he had to do it before the last petal fell from the enchanted rose which the enchantress left with him.

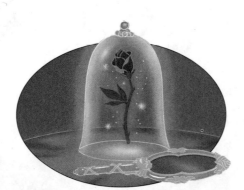

Ashamed of his ugliness, the Beast locked himself away in his castle. A magic mirror was his only window to the outside world.

Not far from the castle lived a beautiful girl named Belle.

Belle loved to read tales of far-off places, magic spells and princes in disguise. She yearned for excitement in her life — and for someone with whom to share it. What she did *not* want was to marry the rude and arrogant Gaston even though Gaston wanted to marry her because she was the most beautiful girl in town.

Belle's father, Maurice, was an inventor, although most of his inventions failed. But whenever Maurice felt like giving up, Belle reminded him about an upcoming fair. "I just know you'll win first prize," she said.

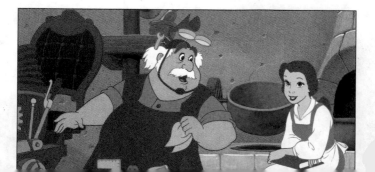

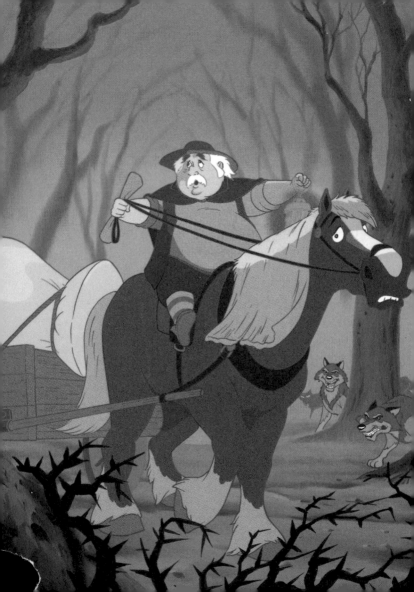

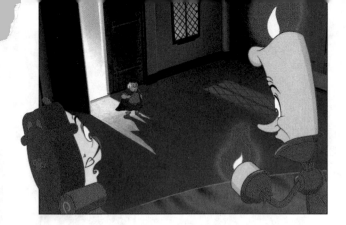

Belle's father finally finished one of his inventions. Then, on his way to the fair, he decided to take a short cut through the woods.

The forest road was dark and scary. When the sound of howling wolves scared his horse, Maurice cried, "Whoa, Phillipe, whoa!" But the terrified horse bolted, and threw his rider.

Maurice had to run from the wolves on foot. Just in time, he stumbled through the gates of the Beast's gloomy castle. No one answered his knock, so he stepped inside the door. "Hello?" he called.

Cogsworth the mantel clock hoped Maurice would go away. But Lumiere the candelabrum called out, "You are welcome here, monsieur."

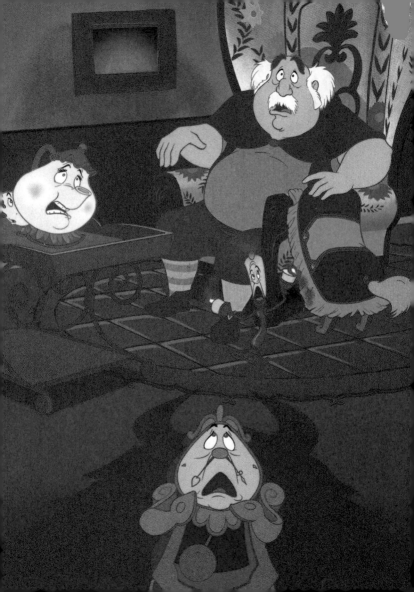

Maurice was astonished to see a talking candelabrum. But soon, he was relaxing in front of a toasty fire, while Mrs. Potts and her son, Chip, served him tea.

Suddenly the Beast's shadow fell over the room. "What are you doing here?" he growled. The next thing Maurice knew, great claws had grabbed him and shut him in a barred cell.

Back in the village, Belle was alone at home, and starting to worry about her father. When Gaston showed up and asked Belle to marry him, Belle politely threw him out of the house.

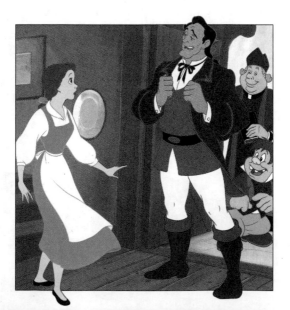

Meanwhile, Phillipe had galloped home to Belle. "Where's Papa? You have to take me to him," Belle cried.

When Lumiere saw Belle enter the castle, he whispered to Cogsworth, "Don't you see? She's the one we've been waiting for. She has come to break the spell!" And he led the girl to her father.

"Oh, Papa! We have to get you out of here!" Belle cried. But just then, the Beast entered.

"Please let my father out. He's sick. Take me instead," Belle pleaded to the massive shape in the shadows.

"Then you must promise to stay here forever," the Beast said.

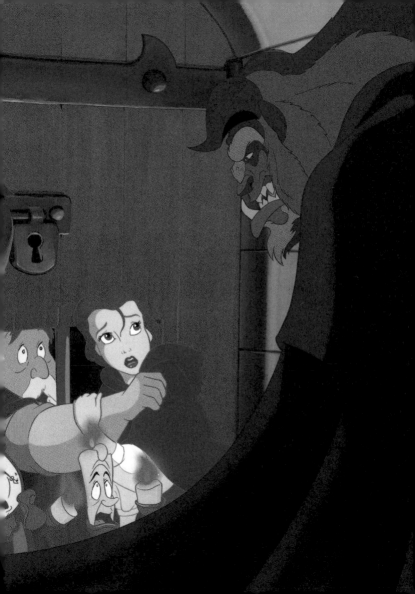

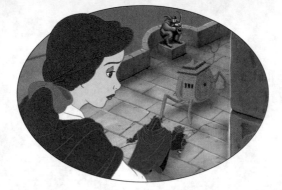

So it was agreed. Belle was heartbroken as she watched her father leave. She had not even been allowed to say good-bye. But she knew she had to keep her promise to the Beast.

Then the wardrobe in her bedroom told her that the Beast wasn't as bad as he seemed. And the food at the castle was delicious. So Belle tried to make the best of things.

Meanwhile, as soon as he returned to their village, Maurice burst into the tavern shouting, "Help! He's got Belle locked in a dungeon!" But when he spoke of "a horrible beast," the villagers decided the old inventor was crazy.

While the others laughed at Maurice, Gaston took his friend Lefou aside. He had thought of a way to try to convince Belle to marry him.

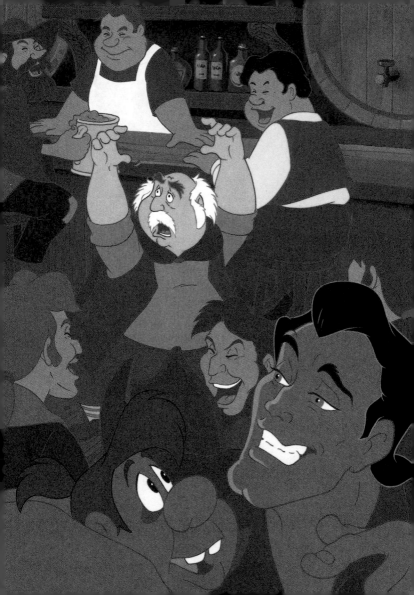

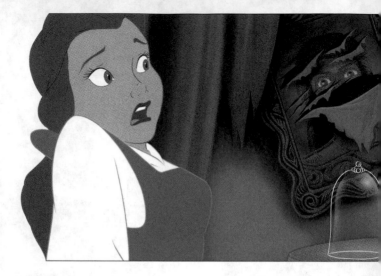

 At the castle, Belle was not locked up at all. The Beast had given her permission to go anywhere she wanted . . . except the West Wing.

Soon, the West Wing was all Belle could think about. So when no one was looking, she crept in. She found a dirty room full of cracked mirrors and broken furniture. The only beautiful, living thing was the enchanted rose, glowing inside a bell jar. Belle was about to touch it, when the Beast roared at her.

"Why did you come here?" he bellowed. "Get out!"

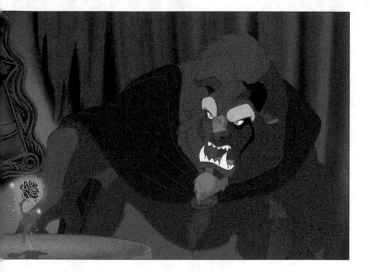

Belle was terrified. Lumiere and Cogsworth saw her as she ran through the halls, but they could not stop her. She ran out the front door. Then she saddled Phillipe, and escaped into the freezing night.

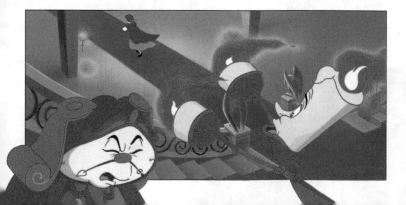

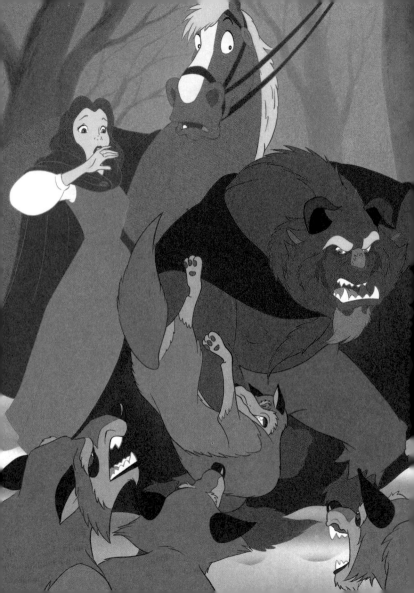

Belle and Phillipe raced through the woods, chased by howling wolves ready to attack. When the horse reared up in fear, Belle was thrown to the ground, and was instantly surrounded by the snarling wolves.

Suddenly, the Beast's giant paw snatched one of the wolves and tossed him through the air. After a fierce battle, the wolves fled whining into the forest. But the Beast had been hurt.

Belle ran to his side and helped him back to the castle.

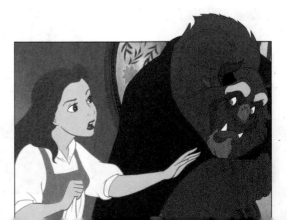

Belle nursed the Beast's wounds until he was better. Before long, Belle and the Beast were reading books, eating meals, and taking walks together.

"Isn't it wonderful!" the enchanted objects agreed as they watched the couple becoming friends.

Finally, the Beast allowed the enchanted objects to dress him in new clothes. "If you care for the girl, you must tell her tonight," Lumiere advised the Beast.

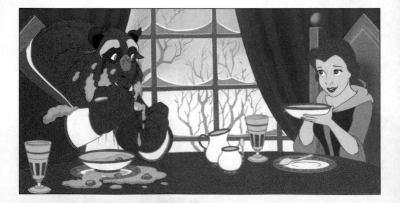

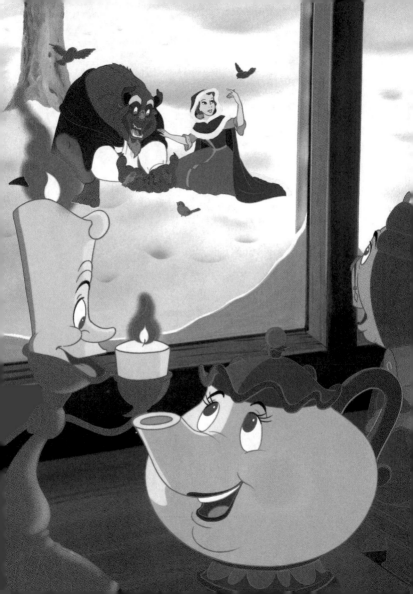

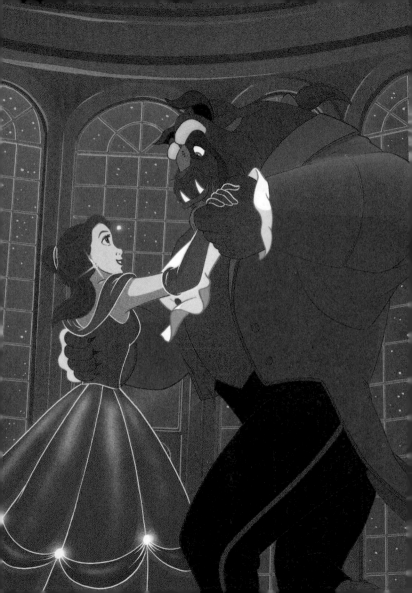

So that night, after dinner, the Beast led Belle into the ballroom and they danced together to a beautiful love song.

"Belle, are you happy here with me?" the Beast asked.

"Yes, but . . . " Belle said, "if only I could see my father, just for a moment."

"There is a way," the Beast told her. And he brought out his enchanted mirror.

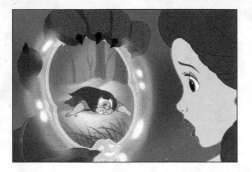

When Belle looked into the mirror, she saw her father lost and shivering in the woods, searching for her. "Oh no! He's sick! He may be dying!" Belle said.

"Then you must go to him," the Beast said. "I release you. But take the mirror with you, so you can look back and remember me."

"How can you let her go?" Cogsworth asked, near tears.

"Because I love her," the Beast replied.

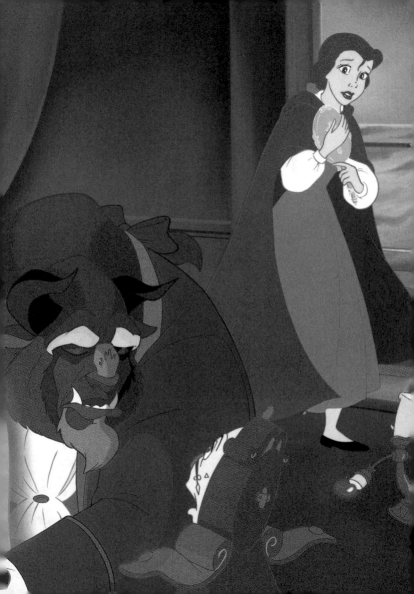

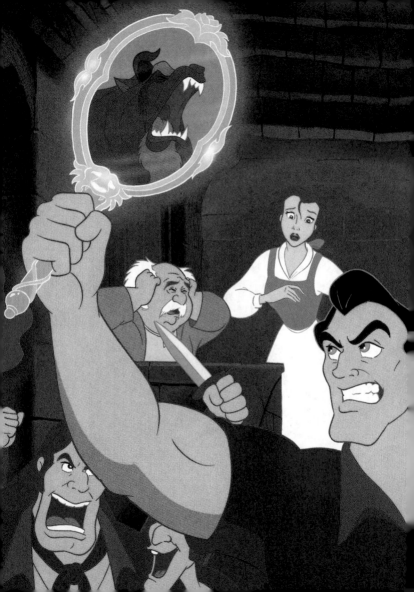

With the mirror's help, Belle found her father and took him home. "How did you escape?" her father asked.

"I didn't, Papa. He let me go. He's changed somehow," Belle said. Just then, there was a knock on the door.

Gaston had brought the director of the insane asylum to lock up Maurice. Gaston hoped he could convince Belle that he was the only one who could save her father — but only if she agreed to marry him.

"My father's not crazy!" Belle protested. Then she held up the magic mirror for the villagers to see. "The Beast is real," she said, "but he's also quite kind."

When the arrogant Gaston realized Belle had feelings for the Beast instead of himself, he snatched the mirror from her. "I say we kill him," he shouted, and he led the excited mob to the Beast's castle.

The household objects put up a brave defense. But the Beast, sure he had lost Belle forever, had no heart for fighting. So when Gaston stormed into his room, the Beast didn't even defend himself.

When Belle arrived seconds later, she saw that Gaston had forced the Beast to the edge of the castle roof.

"No!" Belle screamed.

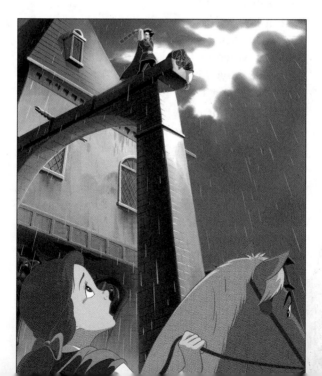

The sound of Belle's voice snapped the Beast into action. He grabbed Gaston by the neck and dangled him over the edge.

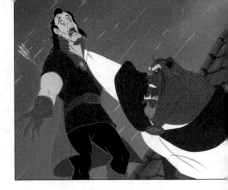

"Let me go! I'll do anything!" Gaston pleaded.

The Beast hesitated for a moment and realized he was not really a beast at heart. He released Gaston, and turned to embrace Belle, who had raced up the stairs.

But as the Beast turned, Gaston pulled a knife from his boot . . . and stabbed the Beast in the back.

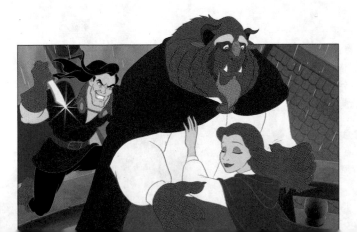

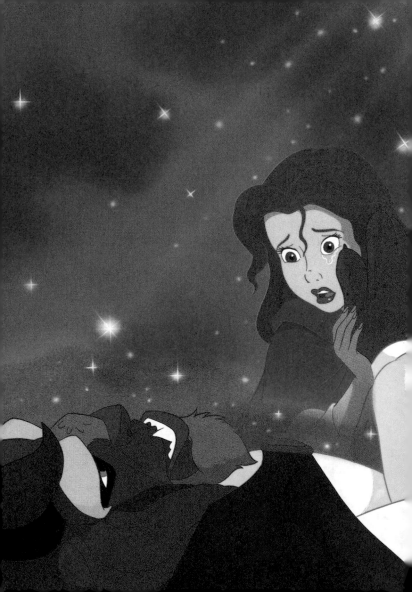

With a howl of pain, the Beast turned on his attacker. Gaston took a frightened step backwards, and plunged from the roof.

But the Beast had been terribly wounded. Belle ran to his side and embraced him. "You came back," the Beast whispered. "At least I got to see you one last time."

"Don't talk like that. You'll be all right," Belle said, fighting back tears.

In the Beast's room, the last petal was about to drop from the rose. "Maybe it's better this way," the Beast said with his last breath.

"No! Please, I love you," Belle sobbed, leaning down to kiss him.

Magically, the Beast rose, and changed back into his human form. "Belle, it's me," said the Prince.

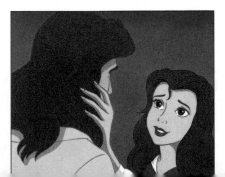

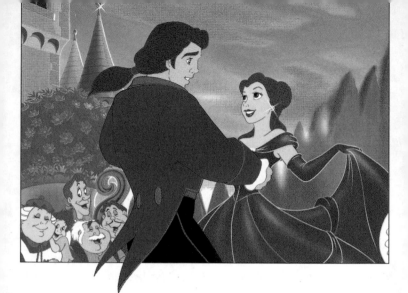

Belle rushed into the Prince's arms. As they
kissed, all the objects in the palace — including
Lumiere, Cogsworth, Mrs. Potts and Chip — were
transformed back into their human forms.

That night, the castle was filled with love as
Belle and the Prince danced and danced, barely
able to take their eyes off each other. And the
castle was once again filled with life and
laughter.

MILAGROS: A BOOK OF MIRACLES

MILAGROS
A BOOK OF MIRACLES

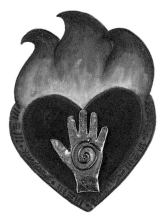

HELEN THOMPSON

ARTWORK BY PADDY BRUCE

HarperSanFrancisco
A Division of HarperCollins*Publishers*

To Charles.
—H.T.

• • •

This book is dedicated to all the miracles through Bill W. and Dr. Bob.
They are good medicine.
—P.B.

Library of Congress Cataloging-in-Publication Data
Thompson, Helen, 1948–
Milagros : a book of miracles / Helen Thompson : artwork by Paddy Bruce. — 1st ed.
p.   cm.
Includes bibliographical references.
ISBN 0-06-251563-2 (cloth)
ISBN 0-06-251579-9 (pbk.)
1. Votive offerings—Latin America—Miscellanea. 2. Spiritual life. 3. Charms. I. Title.
BL570.T46   1998
246'.55—dc21   98–11736

98 99 00 01 02   10 9 8 7 6 5 4 3 2 1

MILAGROS: A Book of Miracles is produced by becker&mayer!, Kirkland, Washington.
www.beckermayer.com

Book design by Trina Stahl • Cover art by Paddy Bruce • Photography by Roger Schreiber
Art direction by Simon Sung • Edited by Lissa Wolfendale
A special thanks to La Tienda, Seattle, Washington for supplying some of the milagros.

CONTENTS

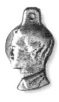

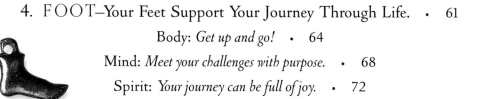
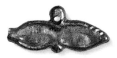

INTRODUCTION

T HE SPANISH WORD *milagro* is usually translated as "miracle." We live today in a world that seems short of miracles, a world where the miracles that do happen go unremarked. Based on traditional Mexican talismans, the tiny, personal charms known as *milagros* remind us that miracles can be small, they can be numerous, and they can happen every day. Often intensely personal, milagros are individual *and* universal, and they offer a way to close the gap between the spiritual and the commonplace.

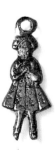

As charming folk art, milagros are talismans against illness, trouble, and pain. But they are more than just a quaint remedy for problems. They are symbolic of a covenant between a believer and a higher spirit, tangible testimony that a promise has been fulfilled—a marriage has been saved, an ailing parent has been restored to good health, a love has been found. Whether you look at their place in your life as a symbol that you are trying something new or as a means to focus yourself on a transition, milagros offer an alternative approach to spirituality.

From the earliest of times, humankind has wanted to communicate with a higher power. We have been giving thanks and propitiation in the form of offerings to gods for thousands of years. The early Sumerians, Persians, Minoans, and Egyptians gave votive gifts depicting animals and people, and evidence of milagros as an ancient custom exists throughout Europe—from Greece, where offerings were given to Aesculapius, the Greek god of healing, north and west into what is now Ireland and Scandinavia. Charms have been offered by such illustrious historical figures as Anne of Austria, who showed her gratitude for

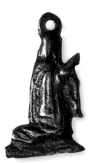

giving birth to an heir to the French throne with a small, winged, silver representation of the infant; and "Hernán Cortés" conqueror of Mexico, who is believed to have presented a gold scorpion emblazoned with emeralds, rubies, and pearls at the shrine of Our Lady of Guadalupe to show his indebtedness for having been saved from a scorpion bite.

Adopted into the rituals of Christianity as a way to thank the saints for answered prayers, the pagan tradition of milagros found its way to the Americas with the Catholic conquistadores. Because the invaders destroyed holy sites throughout the Americas and punished the indigenous peoples for practicing their religion, many traditions of worship have been lost. However, the newly Christianized people of these places took up milagros and their use has continued to endure. Where parts of Guatemala were plagued long ago by pest infestations, grasshopper milagros have been discovered; and the Inca were most likely placing their faith in the fertility of the ground when they planted gold effigies of maize leaves and cobs during sowing festivals. Offerings have been found in as far-flung places as the sacred mounds of Peru, the pyramids of Mexico, the ancient kivas of the American Southwest, and the sacred pools in the Yucatan peninsula.

In Latin America and in areas of the United States where there is a large Hispanic population, offerings are even today a common sight. The little silvery milagros are often found piled in bowls, affixed to crosses with tiny silver nails, or placed at a church altar or a makeshift household shrine. Milagros come in an endlessly

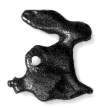 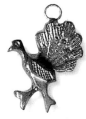 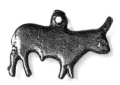

imaginative variety of shapes, sizes, and materials. Sometimes quite sumptuous— bejeweled, elaborately carved, or finely wrought from precious metals—they can be humble, too. Quality has no correlation to sincerity or to outcome. Your milagros are reminders that any act of devotion, no matter how small, is worthy.

That milagros still hold power to affect our troubles testifies to the endurance of a belief system that has eluded repression and destruction to survive for centuries. Perhaps the very modesty of milagros—or their folksy and unassuming status in a complex religious system—has enabled these unsophisticated representations to endure in a modern world wildly and unimaginably different from that which they originated in. Their unthreatening, even whimsical, charm may also account for their increasing popularity in the United States. Engulfed in a mass "pop" culture and sated with consumer goods, we may look at milagros as a way to connect to the durable belief systems of ancient cultures.

The most widely used shapes for milagros are those that represent body parts such as feet, heart, hand, head, and lungs—all those nooks and crannies of the body where ailments settle in and stay. The contemporary interpretation of milagros you'll find in this book (utilizing popular anatomic shapes) is an introduction to the ways and the wisdom of an age-old culture. May learning about these small miracles enhance your life forever.

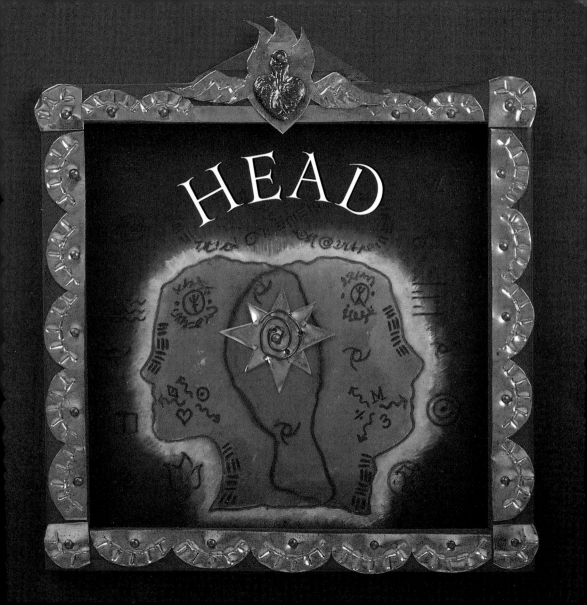

CHAPTER ONE

HEAD

KNOWING IS WISDOM

YOUR HEAD IS your own personal fountain of wisdom. You use it to think and to reason, to plan and to dream.

Head milagros have as much variation as heads do in real life, and represent all ages, shapes, and sizes. Male milagro heads might have beards or mustaches, lots of hair, or be "balding." Milagros of female heads can have distinctive, elaborate hairdos, and some even have earrings. They can be shown in profile, full face, or even in a three-dimensional form.

A photograph can serve as a contemporary version of the head milagro: It is not uncommon to see snapshots of happy infants or smiling husbands and wives placed on statues of favorite saints as a show of gratitude. Sometimes the photo represents the person before calamity struck: a reminder of the state to which the stricken person hopes to return.

El dolor es real cuando usted piensa que lo es.

Pain is real when you think it is.

BODY

Our heads are where our thought processes begin, where we register our pain, and where we consider the sometimes difficult task of asking for help to alleviate the pain. Head milagros are traditionally offered for "real" pain—headaches, memory loss, difficulty learning, and injury or trauma. But they are also offered for more ineffable problems, such as mental illness.

Young and old alike can benefit from the miraculous powers of milagros. A young mother went to a silversmith to have a special milagro made for her baby, who suffered from a tumor on the head. The milagro—accurately representing the large growth on the side of her baby's head—was offered to Saint Francis with a prayer for a cure. Soon after, the tumor disappeared and the grateful mother continued offering head-shaped milagros for a year afterward in gratitude.

If you suffer from infirmities associated with your head, such as headaches, take a moment to think about the message your head is sending you. Aspects of your life are hurting you. If you find that you rush from project to project, worry about what may lie ahead, and toss and turn at night because you can't get the day's problems out of your mind, then it is time to stop and give yourself a mental break.

Use your head milagro as a way to focus on the habits in your life that make it a strain to think a thought through to the end. Think of thought as a limpid river, not as a turbulent and chaotic whirlpool that is drowning you. Avoid using stimulants to energize your thoughts, or depressants to discourage unhappy thoughts. Remember that your thoughts are your head's way of healing itself— learn to listen to yourself thinking, and take your thoughts seriously.

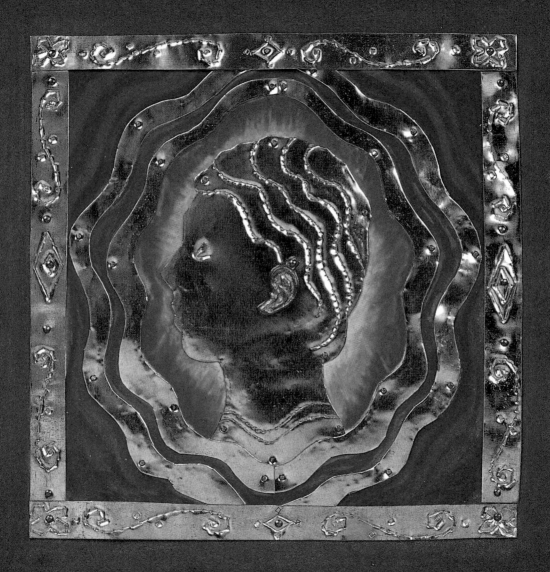

El pensamiento es el modo
qué su cerebro le habla a usted.

Thought is the way your brain talks to you.

MIND

⊱⊰

PAYING ATTENTION TO our thoughts is an activity few of us take seriously. We are more likely to exert our efforts toward suppressing thoughts that come to mind—devaluing them by classifying them as worries, or, if they are pleasant, as daydreams. Placing milagros on shrines or tucking them into the hem of the garment of a favorite saint's statue can be a way to come to terms with unbearable memories and remind yourself to lay those worrying fears to rest.

The folk traditions of milagros, simple expressions occurring in humble sites such as yard shrines or roadside altars commonly seen in the American Southwest, can be an effective method of lifting sadness. Milagros are frequently left at Catholic churches, and sometimes petitioners will show great ingenuity in placing a milagro just where they think it needs to be.

A sterling-silver representation of a woman's head hangs nearly ten feet above the floor on a statue of the Virgin holding the infant Jesus at a church in Tucson, Arizona. The milagro was placed there by a grieving son for his recently departed mother. He had brought a ladder to the church in order to put the milagro in the Virgin's hand, just where he hoped his mother's soul sat on its way to heaven. By going to the trouble of making such a grand gesture, the young man was able to exchange comfort for his grief.

Our minds have capabilities that we often underestimate. When we are worried or depressed, we may be unable to see beyond our troubled mental state. Often, embarrassed by inability to wrest ourselves free from fear and anguish, we are

Anguish is a burden that can be lightened.

unable to seek the help we need. We must remember that, as when the young man bore the little milagro as well as the heavier weight of his own grief up the ladder to place the silver head in the Virgin's hand, the burden of anguish can be lightened. Let the head milagro occupy your thoughts. Use it as a reminder that your mind will tell you the truth.

El conocimiento es mejor
se convierte en sabiduría.

Knowledge is best when it becomes wisdom.

SPIRIT

WE ARE RATIONAL creatures who can think our way into and out of almost any situation. But there are some occasions—and often they are forced on us—when we have no alternative but to seek spiritual assistance. Some of the faithful who offer milagros do so only after they have exhausted every other option. Making a pilgrimage, whether to a shrine or to a place of one's own choice, can be psychologically satisfying simply because it fulfills a need to do "something." Should all else fail, we at least have the satisfaction of knowing that we have tried everything. But keep in mind also that it is a wise person who realizes that to extend one's self to a higher power can enlist the kind of help that comes only with faith. Offering a milagro, or focusing on one in private,

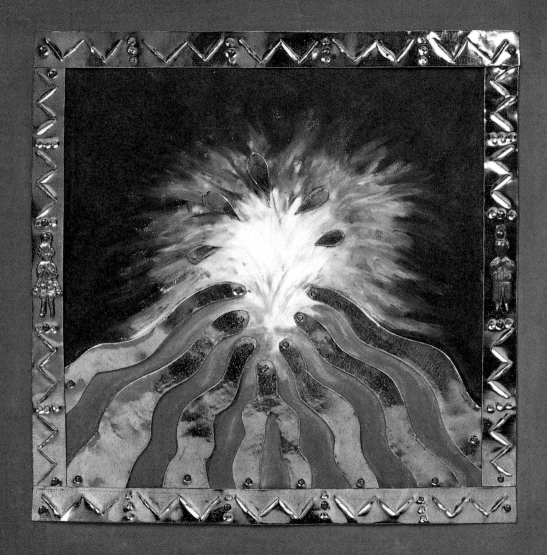

can deepen your commitment to faith. And it can release your mind from the confines of thought.

In Central America, a favorite pilgrimage site is Cartago, the original capital of Costa Rica. The patron saint of Costa Rica is Nuestra Señora de Los Angeles, and a church dedicated to her sits at the base of the Irazu volcano. A little bubbling spring inside the basilica—in a shrine to La Negrita (the Little Black Virgin)—is believed to have curative powers, and the shrine of La Negrita is bedecked with milagros, testimonials, and photographs of those healed by her powers. She is said to have cured sickness and mental derangement and to have averted disasters. Simply the hope of such divine intervention in response to a milagro offering can effect a cure.

There are none among us who have not let our intelligence get the better of us. But when you find yourself under dire circumstances, you should not limit yourself to relying solely on your intelligence; in times of

Use your head milagro to help set your mind free.

spiritual anguish, leave behind your rationality. Use your head milagro to help set your mind free. Accept that your mind can only do so much: Beyond your mind is another realm of expression that you can prepare yourself to receive.

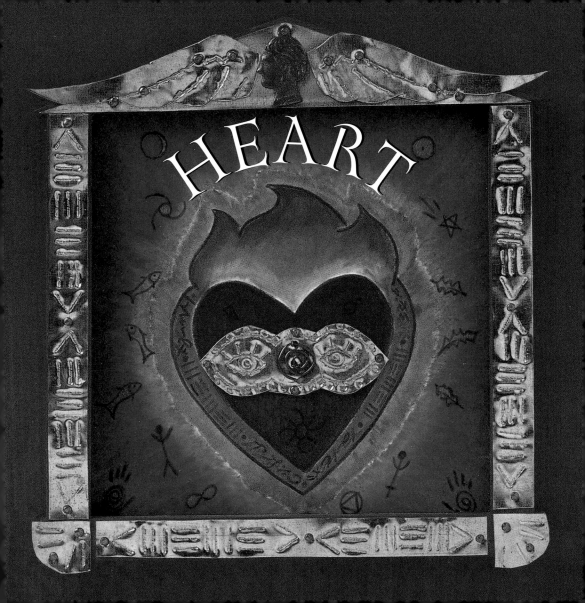

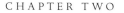

CHAPTER TWO

HEART

HOW WE LOVE

Your heart is sacred. It symbolizes how you love, why you love, who you love. And perhaps more than any other characteristic you have, the *way* that you love defines who you are.

It is no coincidence that, of all the milagros, the heart is the image most commonly offered at shrines. Because we can feel so many levels of pain in our hearts—physical, emotional, and spiritual—supplications for help are often the most heartfelt. But these offerings aren't usually in the shape of the valentine we in the U.S. use as a symbol of the heart—instead, traditional milagros are anatomically correct hearts, sometimes even with blood vessels coursing across the front.

You will see these hearts, even if they are tiny representations of the kind commonly seen in Mexico, pierced by a sword, topped with a rising flame, or encircled with a crown of thorns. Valentine-shaped hearts also come pierced with a sword, usually signifying an unhappy love affair or the loss of a loved one; the image of a rising flame around the heart may be to give thanks for a renewed love or for the discovery of a soul mate.

Si su corazón le duele,
  le está diciendo algo a usted.

If your heart is aching,
  it is telling you something.

BODY

DOES YOUR HEART ache? If your answer is yes, what does this ache mean? If you suffer from ailments associated with your heart—such as heartburn or palpitations—stop and consider what your heart may be saying to you. Listen to your heart and take the message literally: Aspects of your life are causing you pain. Do you find yourself rushing around from the moment you get up in the morning until the minute you close your eyes in sleep at night? You may be grabbing a meal on the run—particularly food that isn't nutritious—and gulping it down without thinking about the effects on your body. Perhaps you are depending on the temporary jolt of caffeine from coffee or chocolate to get you through your daily obligations. As palliatives, fast food and caffeine are merely temporary solutions to a harried lifestyle.

A heart milagro, in addition to symbolizing your love for others, also signifies love and care toward yourself and your own heart. In Latin American countries, you might see a thankful and newly recovered patient wearing a small heart milagro affixed to his or her lapel. Such was the case of a survivor of a heart operation. His prognosis was for only seven more years of life. For those seven years, he wore a heart milagro on the left side of his jacket, over his heart. After seven years had passed and he was blessed with continued robust health, he removed the milagro and donated it to his patron saint.

Look to your heart milagro as a reminder that it is time to quit rushing. Use it to focus. Try eating a pear on a park bench instead of resorting to a candy bar; sit still and listen to your heartbeat for five minutes rather than chug coffee. Hang the milagro where you will see it when you are prone to rush, and you'll remember it carries a message worth slowing down for.

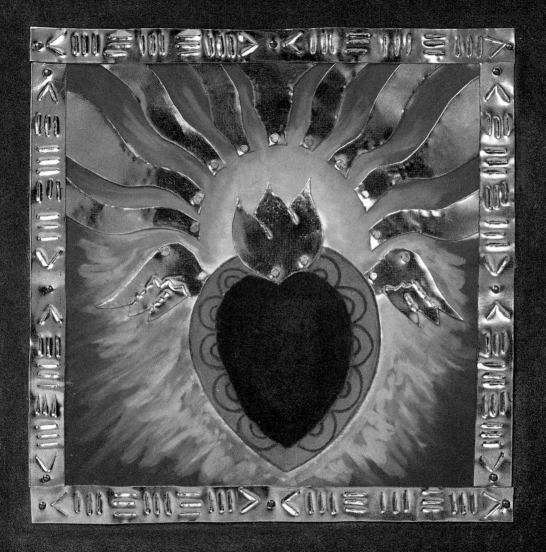

Querer es lo qué su corazón hace mejor.

Loving is what your heart does best.

MIND

❧

LISTEN TO THE message of your heart. Taking this first step will put you on the path to emotional as well as physical health. You can help yourself hear that message and begin healing by putting your worries down in writing. Still a proven way of unburdening the soul, this custom has long been associated with milagros, which often come with notes attached. Carefully composed supplications, painstakingly typed thank-yous, and inscribed photographs of loved ones suggest that the lines of communication between the earthly and the spiritual are open and in working order, with the milagros acting as catalyst.

Sometimes you may simply need to ask for help, like the woman who attached a heartfelt plea of a silver kneeling-woman

Gratitude is an outward-turning gesture.

milagro at a statue of Saint Francis. "Please give me the strength and courage just to keep on going," it read. It is likely that the act of leaving a note on the statue lifted the supplicant's spirits. Sharing our troubles in such a way nearly always lessens the burden of them.

The valentine-shaped heart is the preferred offering for loss of love, whether through death or disaffection. It can also be a symbol of thanksgiving for a love restored.

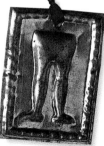

Hospitals run by the Catholic Church usually have statues of saints somewhere on the premises, and it is not uncommon to find clusters of milagros piled at their bases or to see them draped with ribbons glittering with sewn-on milagros.

One young woman continued to offer heart milagros each year on the anniversary of her husband's recovery from a near-fatal tractor accident on their farm.

She had brought the first heart the night of his devastating mishap shortly after their wedding—placing it in the outstretched hand of a statue of Saint Francis—and she had promised to continue giving thanks if her husband's life were spared. His injuries were so crushing that both wife and doctors admitted only a miracle could restore her husband to good health. But her wish was granted, and her annual offerings of milagros represent her ongoing gratitude and acknowledgment of the magnitude of the gift.

You may know in your heart that the capacity to show gratitude is different from just being grateful. But you might be too busy to pay attention to your emotions. Gratitude is an outward-turning gesture that includes others. Show gratitude when you can, and leave some evidence along the way. Take this heart milagro to heart, and use it as a reminder that the effects of love can be tangible.

Comparta lo qué lleva en su corazón.

Share what you have in your heart.

SPIRIT

THE LOVE YOU can give to a higher spirit is one of the great gifts of life. It seems more commonplace in less-developed areas of the world, but belief shouldn't be mistaken for lack of sophistication. Sharing the spirit of yourself with others augments and enriches your life and the lives of those around you. Communal gestures of faith, such as the pilgrimage of the Saint Francis feast-day celebration in the American Southwest—for which pilgrims arrive by foot or in rickety autos and wait in sweltering heat to make their offerings—have a value you can only experience by participating.

Throughout the Americas there are sites where the faithful have come for many years—some by foot, some on their knees for

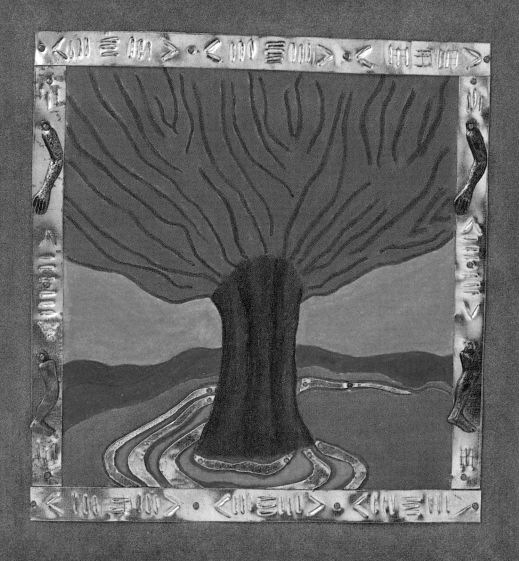

the last few blocks of their pilgrimage—to pay homage to a saint for a prayer answered. In Tlaxcala, Mexico, pilgrims have offered so many heart milagros to the Virgin at the Basilica of Our Lady of Ocotlan, that the enormous five-point star behind this larger-than-life statue is completely covered.

The power of devotion can also be seen at the ancient shrine of Our Lord of Chalma in Mexico. Pilgrims to the shrine, which honors a black Christ figure much loved in the area, always stop at a huge cypress tree out of which curative waters are said to flow. The tree is lavishly hung with milagros testifying to the restorative powers of the waters. Crutches, umbilical cords, driver's licenses, and limb-shaped milagros vie for space with heart milagros and snapshots of children rescued from death's grasp. Since milagros are often offered after a prayer has been answered, so much evidence is a public testament to the power of faith—the sight alone of such faith can deepen belief.

Then there are individual examples of acts of faith: A middle-aged daughter was grieving intensely over the death of her mother, to whom she had been very close. Because her heart felt as if it would break, the daughter offered heart milagros at the shrine she had built in honor of her mother in her back yard. Finally she decided to bury the heart milagros, and when the flowers began to bloom in her yard, she believed the happy profusion was a response from her mother.

Popular psychology, too, attests to the value of sharing your hopes and dreams with those around you. All of us have allowed the insidious cynicism of modern life to affect us in some way: We may yell at other drivers in traffic, or we may do worse and yell at someone we love. It will do your heart good to put something else first in your life besides yourself and to relearn the value of belief. Your heart milagro is a memento of the commonality of faith.

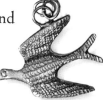

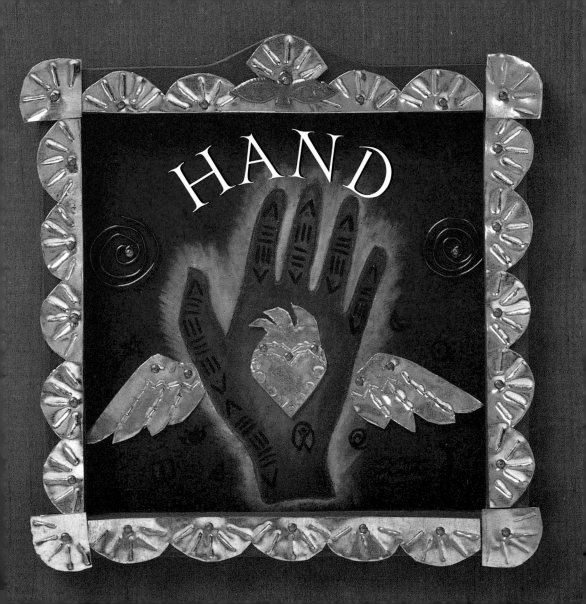

CHAPTER THREE

HAND

YOUR HANDS CONNECT YOU
TO OTHERS

YOUR HANDS ARE the way you relate to the world: how you reach out to others and how others return your touch; what you use to do work; and often, they are the instruments through which your creativity flows to create music, art, or poetry.

The clenched fist is a sign of good luck in Brazil and other parts of Latin America, where hand milagros are ubiquitous. In the United States and Mexico, hand milagros nearly always come in the shape of the back of a single hand that ends at the wrist or is completed by a fancy cuff. The fingers of the milagro are usually extended with the joints and fingernails depicted. In the event of a devastating injury, the afflicted part is highlighted with a different metal or shown defined by a ragged edge. Occasionally, both hands are shown, with fingertips touching as if in prayer.

Tocar es el bálsamo para aliviar el dolor.

Touch is the balm to ease pain.

BODY

OUR HANDS ARE essential to making a living—without his hands, a craftsman can't make his crafts, an artist can't create, a laborer can't work, and a factory employee can't produce. Milagros of the hand are common in societies where the well-being of families depends on physical labor, and in our own highly technological one, hands provide the means for survival—both physical and spiritual. Hands are the connection to others that gives us our humanity, and may be why phrases like "lending a hand" evoke a sense of the importance of giving something of yourself.

An older Mexican-American woman used hand milagros both to aid her own work ethic and to seek a divine helping hand. Her neighbor who lived in a house that she loved came to see her one

You have the ability to ease someone else's pain.

day and told her that he was going to sell his house and give her the first chance to buy it. He added that he would give her a week to get the money together to make the purchase. The woman felt sure no bank would give her a loan, so she offered a hand milagro to Saint Francis with a prayer that she would work hard in her job as a maid to repay a loan. Three days later, she found a bank to loan her the money to buy the house she had always loved.

If you are experiencing problems with your hands, such as aching in the joints or tendinitis, it may be time to consider how your work is affecting your life. Some aspect of the way you make your living may be unhealthy. Repetition, overuse, or inflexibility can cause physical symptoms that reveal emotions or attitudes long hidden or as yet unacknowledged.

Take a moment to think about your hands

and what you use them for:
Place them in your lap, with the
fingers of one hand lightly touching the fingers of the other. Close
your eyes and envision your hand
milagro as a manifestation of your
hands at work. Remember another of
your hands' capabilities: the healing
power of touch. With every touch, you
have the ability to help ease someone
else's pain.

Sus manos son para bienvenir a otros,

Your hands are for welcoming others,

MIND

ও৩

JUST AS YOU use your hands to greet new people you meet
with a firm shake, you can also use them to introduce new and
satisfying elements and to rewelcome those whom you already
know into a more intimate role in your life.

In the American Southwest as far back as the late 1700s, milagros were necessities in a well-run Hispanic household. The small
silver amulets were usually pinned to a statue or hung on a paint-
ing of the family's favorite saint, and it was a thoughtful host who
kept a supply on hand (stored in miniature velvet-covered caskets)
for family members or friends in need. Taking a trip across the
border to replenish a depleted supply of milagros was a gesture of
kindness that one might offer, and in this way, milagros themselves

have come to show a way to reach out to loved ones and those in need.

Begin to think of your hands as being more than the necessary means to earning a living—limiting your hands to this function alone also limits yourself. The effect can be crippling to your whole being.

Visualize other uses for your hands, such as grasping the hand of a friend, holding a pet or a baby, planting a favorite flower, or writing a poem. These are welcoming acts that will bring friends, beauty, and inspiration into your life. In fact, giving a milagro to a friend can be a good way of telling him or her you are lending a hand.

Gestures of friendship and caring can be as comforting as a touch. When we are in pain, it is easy to overlook how egocentric and self-involving pain can be—reaching out to someone else in pain

Reaching out to someone else in pain is often the best balm.

is often the best balm. Think of your hands as your way of guiding other people into your life. Just as the thoughtful householder kept a cache of milagros to hand out to those in need, your own supply of milagros or just your goodwill can be at the ready too. A life not shared is a life of loneliness—let the hand milagro remind you that friends are the most important component of a happy and productive life.

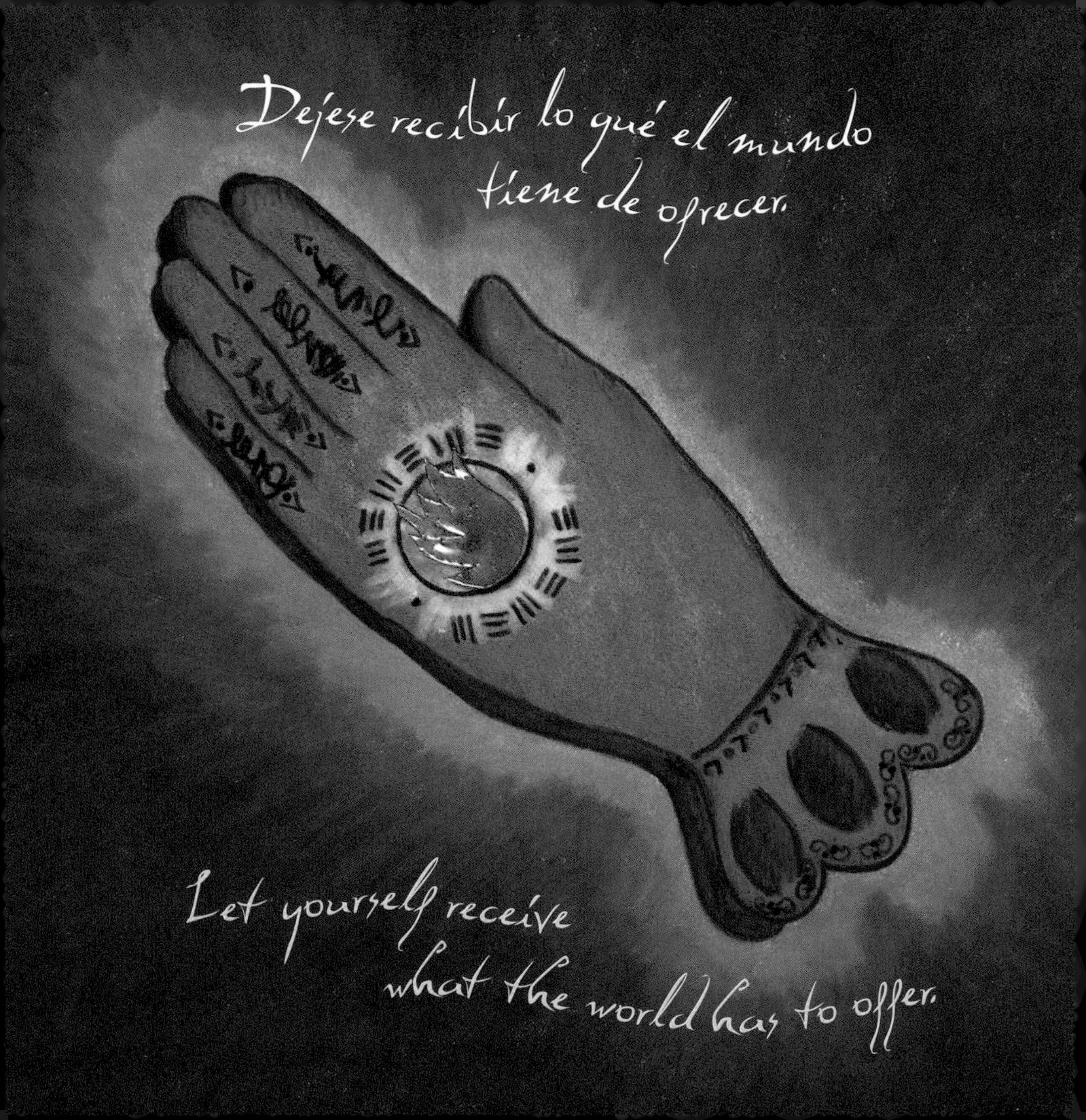
Dejese recibir lo qué el mundo tiene de ofrecer.
Let yourself receive what the world has to offer.

SPIRIT

MOST OF US like to think of ourselves as being independent and capable. But depending only on yourself in times of turmoil and uncertainty can be overwhelming. Opening your hands and your heart is a gesture of faith that can be rewarding.

Milagros serve a dual function: They are used by the grateful to offer thanks for answered prayers, and by supplicants to ask for divine aid. On the Island of Margarita, off the coast of Venezuela where the waters in the area once harbored a productive pearl field, sailors and pearl divers pay homage to the Virgin del Valle. Her sanctuary in the village of El Valle is filled with votive offerings and pearl-encrusted milagros of hands and legs, essential tools in pearl diving. The families pray for good catches and safe returns.

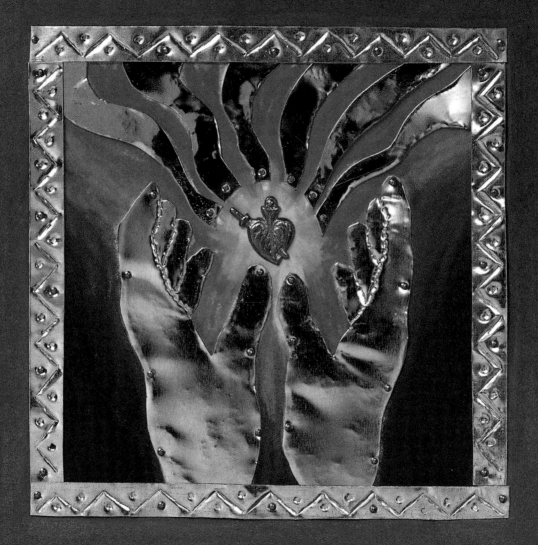

Desperation can prepare you to receive comfort.

These prayers are more than requests for a favor—by asking for help, the supplicants admit and share their need for divine intervention and, by doing so, expose their deepest vulnerabilities.

Fear of being abandoned, of being cast out, and of death are primal, no matter how civilized the society we live in or our season of life. We all experience periods in our lives when events are not in our control. It is under these dire circumstances that we are reminded that we cannot always have our way, solve a problem, maneuver a desirable outcome, or prevent a tragic consequence. Turning to a higher power—opening our hands to another source of strength—can be the final resort of the desperate. Ironically, that very desperation can prepare you to receive comfort.

Even friends and relatives can help pray for something a loved one really needs—this form of spiritually lending a hand strengthens a person's resolve and involves in the recovery process those closest to the ailing person and the supplicant. A distraught father asked his family and friends to help him ask for a miracle when his baby son was injured in a car wreck. After a week, the child emerged from his coma to see the happy faces of parents and relatives grouped around him.

Offering a milagro can be a simple and tangible way to receive consolation from a higher power. Milagros are symbols of a request for assistance; use yours as a way to find new strength. Asking for help is the most wondrous way to receive support.

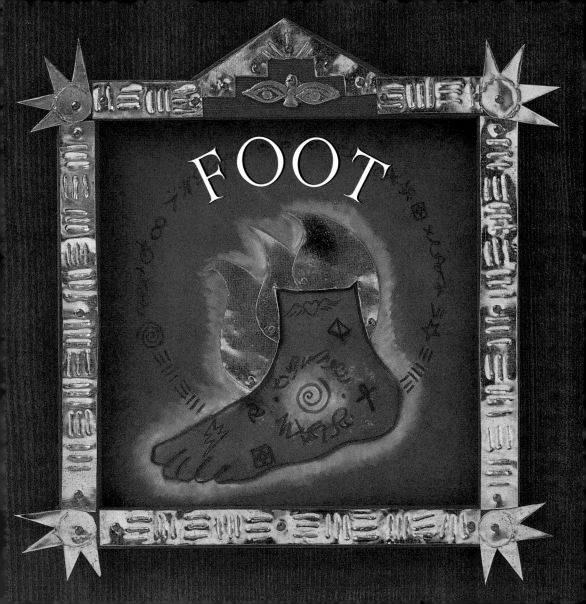

FOOT

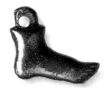

CHAPTER FOUR

FOOT

YOUR FEET SUPPORT YOUR
JOURNEY THROUGH LIFE

Your feet are the foundation upon which your whole body rests and relies. They act as your transportation; they must bear the daily weight of your body; and despite being so sturdy, they are among the most sensitive areas of the body.

Like hands, feet are indispensable in cultures whose economies are dependent upon physical labor. Foot milagros frequently show up at pilgrimage sites—in part because many of the penitent have arrived after having walked for sometimes hundreds of miles. These milagros can appear as life-size wood renditions complete with toenails and wrinkles at the joints, or as tiny silver versions that detail such ailments as flat feet. They have been found in the ancient locations of the Etruscan period in Italy and in centuries-old sites in Catholic southern Germany, where offering milagros was a popular custom among the peasantry.

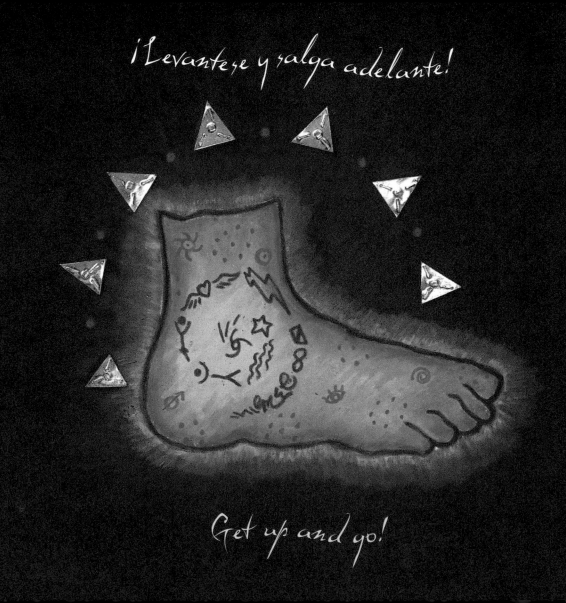

BODY

ARE YOUR FEET in pain? Foot problems can be some of the most distressing, and when severe, these difficulties can be literally immobilizing. If you are plagued with foot problems, it may be time to ponder what your pain stands for: If you notice that you are standing too much at work or at play, never giving yourself a moment to sit down and relax, then perhaps it is time for you to slow down. Or perhaps there are some things in your life that it is time to walk away from—and that is exactly what feet are for.

The Afro-Brazilians and the Native peoples in northeast Brazil share certain beliefs from which we could stand to learn. They believe disease and misfortune are the result of intangible forces

If you are persistent, you will always end up in a better place.

invading the body, and that offering milagros is a way to cast out misfortune.

Focus on your own foot milagro as a way to walk away from unnecessary unhappiness. Muster your inner strength to visualize a goal that you can proceed toward— your foot milagro can show you that path. Remember that placing one foot in front of the other has a cumulative effect: If you are persistent, you will always end up in a better place.

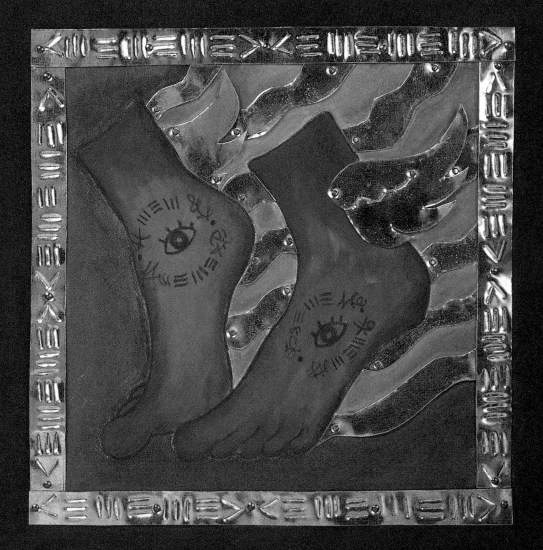

Encuentre sus desafíos con propósito.

Meet your challenger with purpose.

MIND

WE OFTEN ENDOW problems with more power than they actually have by thinking of them abstractly, thus making them seem too unwieldy for us to get a handle on them. To get past these inhibitors, you must first take notice of your frustrations. But sometimes just the act of noticing can stop a person in their tracks. Don't let that happen to you. Think of acknowledging your problems as the first step toward moving past them—not to run away, but to find a deliberate method of considering a new path and following it.

The act of offering a milagro—even if it is in your own private ceremony—can be a way to look for that new path. It is commonly observed that pilgrims feel invigorated by the pilgrimage and their

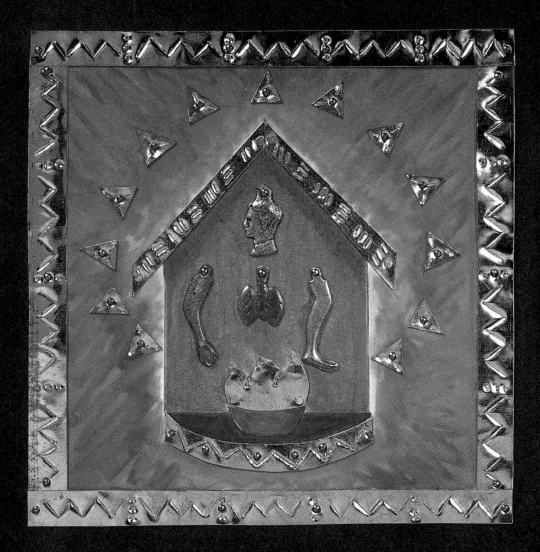

resolve is strengthened. By making an offering, you open a path for new dialogue, whether it is with yourself or with a higher spirit.

It is a spiritual failing of modern culture that it is too easy for us to think of ourselves as alone in the world. Across the American Southwest and Latin America, milagro offerings found in places as diverse as roadside chapels, wall niches, and shrines of neighborhood grocery stores, hospitals, and public spaces reaffirm that, indeed, we are not alone; many are attempting to instigate such a dialogue. Use your foot milagro as a reminder that certain ideas—such as the belief in a higher power—have universality. Use it as a token to inspire you to seek new paths. Looking for a new way can be like making your own pilgrimage—your journey will always lead to self-discovery and self-acceptance, the two greatest challenges life presents.

Su jornada puede estar llena de felicidad.

Your journey can be full of joy.

SPIRIT

RECOGNIZE THE WORTH of each individual step of your life. Having an ultimate objective is in itself a necessary and valuable thing, but by focusing overly upon a far-away—and oftentimes unreasonable—goal, we risk missing out on the delights offered by the day-to-day.

Making a pilgrimage is one of the great traditions associated with the offering of milagros. The pilgrim who brings a milagro to a saint's statue or to a pilgrimage site is completing the final rite of a personal religious act. But the pilgrimage actually begins long before the first step is taken, with the decision to seek supernatural help.

Every October, near the town of Magdalena in Mexico, it is common to see Mexican and Indian pilgrims trudging along wagon paths, through the mountains, and across the desert in the cool of the night to reach the San Francisco chapel there. They carry with them powerful tokens of their belief— holy pictures, little statues of Saint Francis, meaningful personal mementos from their households—to rub against the statue of San Francisco.

During this fiesta, an atmosphere of celebration and gaiety pervades the streets of Magdalena: Makeshift food stands sell fresh coffee, hot tortillas, and grilled meat, while vendors hawk balloons, jewelry,

Contemplate where life can take you if you let it.

clothing, and religious souvenirs to the beat of the mariachi bands that stroll through the *calles*. As rich and poor, healthy and sick, sacred and profane mix together, the event soon transcends the strictly religious to encompass an even broader meaning—the universality of experience.

Use your foot milagro to contem-plate where life can take you if you let it. Think of your journey as being like a pilgrimage—difficult and even treacherous, but a trip that can also be full of joy. Learn to think of the act of

Think of your journey as being like a pilgrimage.
traveling as the valuable component of your pilgrimage. Look at
your foot milagro and remind yourself to enjoy making your way
through life—that the journey itself is what matters.

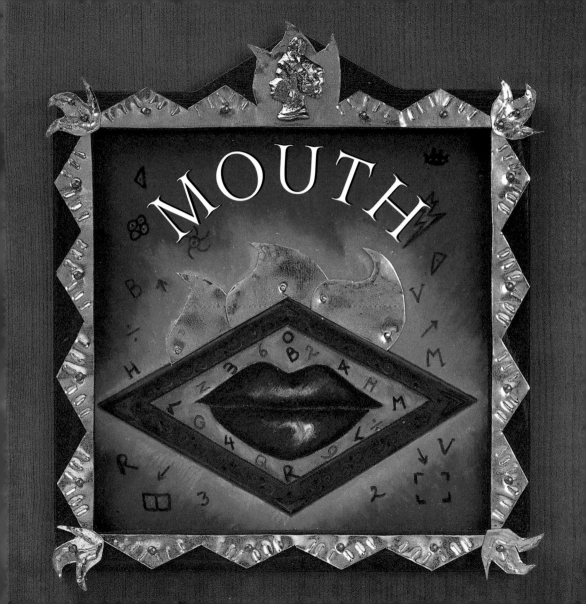

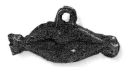

CHAPTER FIVE

MOUTH

OUR WORDS ARE AS GOOD
AS OUR DEEDS

OUR MOUTHS ARE the portals out of which we express
our thoughts and feelings, and through which we receive
our daily sustenance. Remember that your mouth is the way
you communicate with your body. Stay healthy by eating nutritious food, speaking well of others, and knowing when to say
nothing at all.

Mouth milagros often are representations of straight and

perfectly formed teeth and gums. These milagros are offered for aid in tooth diseases such as cavities and decay, which can be portrayed by engraving along the gum area of the milagro. Sometimes sets of dentures are found at sacred sites; but, considering the importance of a good set of teeth, it is likely that such gifts are made after the wearer's death, in gratitude for a happy life.

In milagros tradition, representations of mouths and lips are rarer than those of other body parts, since diseases and misfortunes associated with areas such as the heart and feet usually command more attention. But even though lip milagros are a rarity, the lips still play a major role: One of the most affecting customs associated with presenting a milagro is the kiss, either to the milagro itself or to the saint's statue. It is quite common to see a petitioner present an offering, say a silent prayer, and then kiss the milagro. As a farewell gesture or as a very personal way of sealing a promise, the kiss expresses our deepest emotions and personalizes our faith.

Su boca es para comunicarse.

Your mouth is for communicating.

BODY

I F YOU ARE plagued by ailments of the gums, teeth, or mouth, take some time to consider what these problems may be telling you about your life. Are you doing your part to keep your mouth free from tooth decay and gum disease by eating nutritious foods? Or do you grab quick snacks of sugary foods because you don't have time to sit down to a real meal? You may be so rushed during the day that at night, even when you are asleep, you are stressed out. Teeth-grinding is a painful result of unresolved anxiety.

Mouth milagros have been used to cure more tangible problems as well as anxiety-created ones. A woman in her mid-forties wanted desperately to become pregnant, so she offered milagros and prayed to the Virgin Mary. The woman eventually became pregnant and

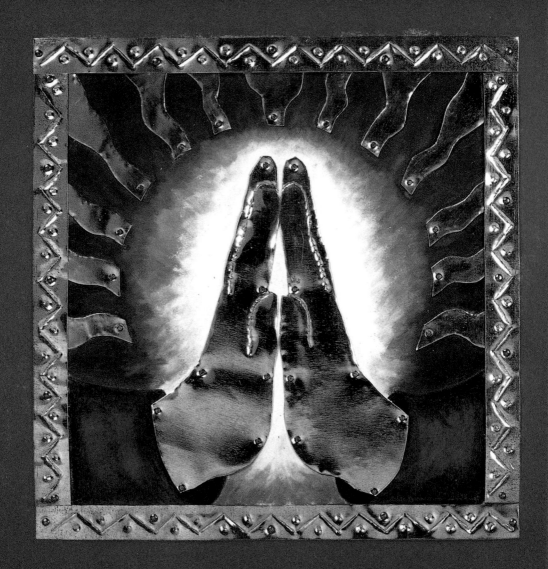

Your mouth is the way you communicate with your body.

had a little boy, but his jaw was malformed. Convinced that she had received something she shouldn't have asked for, the woman began offering mouth milagros to the Virgin every week. After six months, a surgical team from the United States visited her village and offered to repair her son's deformity. The woman remains convinced that her prayers would not have been answered had she not been persistent and generous with her milagros.

Look to your mouth milagro as a symbol of the sacred trust you have to your own body. Use it to focus: Sit quietly at your dining table and contemplate the meal you are about to eat. Ensure that you remain healthy by making sure the food you eat is nutritious. Hang the mouth milagro where you can see it when you eat and

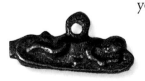 you will remember that your mouth is the way you communicate with your body—be nice to yourself and keep yourself healthy.

El hablar sin cuidado
puede lastimarle a usted y a otros.

Careless talk can hurt yourself and others.

MIND

LANGUAGE IS ONE of our most powerful tools; give your own words the same sanctity a prayer would have, and employ them just as carefully. Just as in prayer, your words should aim to bring joy, solace, or knowledge.

Listening to yourself talk is an easy way to discover the message you are sending out to the world. Don't forget that what you say is a potent reminder to others of your thoughts and beliefs—even if you don't consider what you are saying to be important, someone else might. Never underestimate the effect your words may have. Use your mouth milagro as a reminder of the power of speech.

Plagued by a compulsion to gossip and speak ill of nearly everyone, a young man turned to prayer and offering mouth milagros to achieve spiritual peace. He offered them daily, using the time to meditate on the effects of ill-will and the benefits of goodwill. He began to look forward to his daily offerings as a time to reflect. After some months, he began to think better of himself as well as of others. He no longer harbored negative thoughts about the world around him—he attributed his newfound mental health to the act of offering.

So powerful is language that many milagros are offered with a written prayer or message attached. The writing of such a letter may help to unburden the author's soul, but another benefit of putting these prayers to paper is undoubtedly the sense of communion with an unseen power. To leave a message is to initiate what can be an intensely spiritual conversation, for others as well as the author. Long typewritten letters detailing the saga of a petitioner's troubles can often be seen hanging from a statue of a saint or

Focus on the effect your words have on the rest of the world.

affixed to a roadside shrine. Sometimes these letters describe the miracle of deliverance from dire circumstances. The chronicler expects the letter to be read—potentially both by a higher power and by others seeking miraculous testimony.

Expect your own words to be heard by passersby as well as by a higher power. Remind yourself that offhand remarks can cut, that carelessly offered opinions don't contribute to the overall good, and that deliberate meanness is inexcusable. Use your mouth milagro to focus on the effect your words have on the rest of the world, whether it is the small, personal world you inhabit or the larger world around you. Just as in prayers where you wish well for someone in trouble or pain, your words should aim to bring joy, solace, or knowledge. Remember that the act of conversing is a kind of communion—engage in it with respect.

Palabras bondadosas durarán para siempre.

Kind words will last forever.

SPIRIT

MAKE A VOW with yourself: Be the first to say something kind today; resist the urge to make hurtful remarks; learn to say what needs to be said. Most important, learn to talk to yourself in a way that reflects your belief that your words can make things better.

In many parts of Latin America and the American Southwest, supplicants accompany their offerings of milagros with a vow, a promise between that person and a higher power that is sealed with the presentation of the milagro. Although this is a folk custom and not officially sanctioned by formal religion, it is often performed in conjunction with Catholic ritual, accompanied by conventional Catholic prayers, devotional gifts, and lighting of candles. But the vow can be made informally, particularly in times of crisis when attending to formalities may be the last thing on the promiser's mind.

We have all felt the despair and hopelessness that seem inevitable components of living in the modern world. Making a pact with a 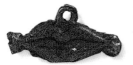 higher power is the manifestation of your faith in the existence of a power beyond yourself, and expresses both the hope of divine intervention and the belief that such intervention is possible. You need only ask for help to receive it.

Regard your mouth milagro as a way to express what you only dare to hope for. It is a way to extend your thoughts and words out into the world, where they will work for the common and spiritual good. Remember that expressions of faith work like self-fulfilling prophecies—the very act of expressing becomes the act of faith. Look to your milagro as a way to reconfirm and restate your connection with spiritual power. Use it to focus on ways to continue the conversation.

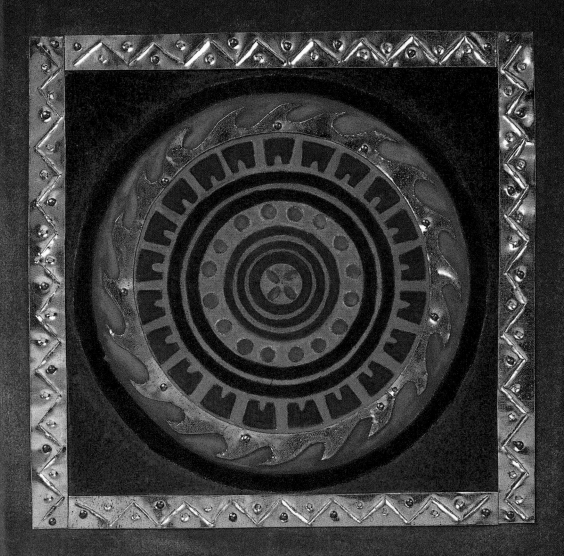

MAKING YOUR OWN MILAGROS

HISTORICALLY, MILAGROS HAVE been made from many different materials—the earliest from wood, rock, clay, bone, and local materials such as amber. More modern milagros have been fashioned from gold, silver, copper, bronze, and tin. Since many milagros are intensely personal, a petitioner might bring a piece of jewelry, a coin, or a favorite household object to be melted down and remade into an offering for a special occasion. As individualistic as they are and as creative as some of the artists who made them were, milagros almost never bear a hallmark or an artist's signature, an intriguing characteristic that makes these wonderful offerings seem to belong to anyone and everyone.

Give your own milagros personal and private meaning by making them yourself. First find a pattern or symbol—such as a heart, or a flower, or the sun—that holds particular meaning for you. If you are still searching for symbols, let your imagination wander until one presents itself. Trace the pattern with a pencil on a translucent sheet of paper, and transfer the pattern to a heavy sheet of paper, such as Kraft paper or colored construction paper. To further personalize the milagro, apply symbols or colors with watercolors, felt-tip pen, or glue-on stickers. Cut out the pattern and, if you want to preserve it, laminate it. Punch a hole in the top of the milagro and insert a colorful ribbon. Tie the ribbon in a bow and hang the milagro where it will remind you of the message you want to send yourself.

BIBLIOGRAPHY

Egan, Martha. *Milagros: Votive Offerings from the Americas.* Santa Fe: Museum of University of New Mexico Press, 1991.

Hay, Louise L. *Heal Your Body: The Mental Causes for Physical Illness and the Metaphysical Way to Overcome Them.* Carlsbad, California: Hay House, 1994.

Minneapolis Institute of Arts, and Walker Art Center. *American Indian Art: Form and Tradition.* New York: E.P. Dutton, 1973.

Myss, Caroline. *Why People Don't Heal and How They Can.* New York: Harmony Books, 1997.

Oktavec, Eileen. *Answered Prayers: Miracles and Milagros Along the Border.* The University of Arizona Press, 1995.

ABOUT THE AUTHOR
AND THE ILLUSTRATOR

HELEN THOMPSON is an editor and writer for *Metropolitan Home* and the author of the *In Celebration* series, books that offer a wealth of indulgences for every season. She was a writer and editor at *Texas Monthly* for seventeen years, and the former managing editor of *Domain,* an arts and lifestyle magazine. She has written for *Worth, Men's Journal,* and *Southern Style.* She lives in Austin, Texas.

A native of the Pacific Northwest region, PADDY BRUCE was born in Victoria, British Columbia in Canada. Her art education and background have taken her to design school in London, Mexico City, and San Miguel de Allende in Mexico where she first discovered milagros and the diverse arts of Mexican culture. A graduate of Western Washington University in Bellingham, Washington, she is currently a "Bellinghamster"; here she resides, works, exhibits, and sails in and around the Puget Sound region and points farther north.